ZULU

Story by Doris Dube

Illustrated by Tomy Ndebele

Design and Color by Geoffrey Isley

ZULU

Story by Doris Dube

Illustrated by Tomy Ndebele

Design and Color by Geoffrey Isley

Published as part of the
Centennial Celebration of
Brethren in Christ World Missions

Published by the Board for World Missions
of the Brethren in Christ Church
in cooperation with Evangel Publishing House

©1997 by Brethren in Christ World Missions

ISBN 0-916035-78-6
Library of Congress Catalog No. 96-79003

GLOSSARY

Pg.   1.   Zulu: a name meaning rain, also the Ndebele name for heaven.

Pg.   3.   Zenzo: a name meaning deeds.

Pg.   4.   *ENdlovu eNyathi*: customary way of saying thank you.
            After meals this means, "Father thank you for the food."
            "Mother thank you for the food." Here family names are used.
            Other surnames are used in another village.

Pg.   9.   *Gogo:* grandmother.

Pg.   13.   *Isitshwala:* a thick porridge made of corn meal, a staple food.
            Amasi: sour milk – rather thick – used as a relish.

Pg.   14.   *Isikhukhukhu:* a special tree, with slimy bark and leaves,
            especially used for rock sliding.

Pg.   17.   *Khokho:* great-grandmother.

Pg   19.   Groundnut: Some people call it monkey nut.
            North Americans call it peanut.

Pg.   21.   *Gogola:* a special endearment for grandmother.

pg.   23.   *Mfundisi:* a term of respect given to male preachers and missionaries.

It was nine years ago.

Mother was at Mtshabezi Mission Hospital.

She had been waiting for almost nine months

for me to come.

I was born in the middle of the night.

The next day the first heavy rains fell.

They called me **Zulu,** which means rain.

The nights are always short.

I hear Mother's voice.

"Wakey, wakey sleepy-head.

The sun is up.

You'll be late for school.

Quick. Get up. Get out of bed.

Look at the sky.

Look at the sun.

The day is ready to greet you."

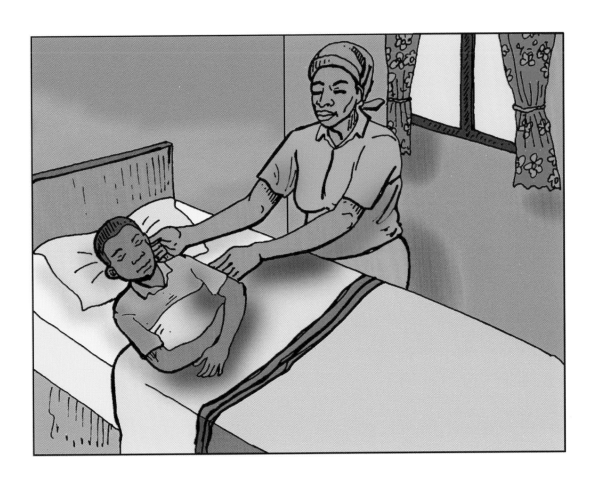

I am in Grade 5.

My brother Zenzo and I go to

Induba Government Primary School.

After school we usually help mother

in the house or garden.

Afterwards we do our homework, then play.

I am lucky I go to school.

My grandmother never did.

Her father did not think girls should

learn to read or write.

Father is a bus driver.

He has been to many places on his bus.

Some days he does not go to work.

People bring their cars, lorries and trucks

to our backyard. Father fixes them.

Usually Zenzo and I watch him.

Mother does not go out to work.

She looks after our house.

She cooks our food, sews and mends our clothes.

She makes life comfortable for all of us.

Father loves Mother's cooking and always says,

"Thank you, beautiful cook - wonderful food."

We just say, *"ENdlovu eNyathi."*

Sunday – our day for Sunday school. Yipey!

It's a long walk to Mpopoma Church.

Should we miss a day? Oh no!

Our teacher, Mrs. Zama Ncube, tells many

interesting stories about God.

Such lovely pictures too.

We just love to sing.

"Woz'eSunday school."
  (Come to Sunday school.)

"Zonk'isont'ek'seni,"
  (Every Sunday morning)

"Woz'eSunday school."
  (Come to Sunday school.)

I travel with Mother.
We go to a big meeting for
the whole church.
It is called a conference.
It is at a mission station.

Many people come to the
conference.
I go to help look after the
baby.

NGUBANI

UMAKHE

The meetings are long.

The people talk and talk.

The children have special activities.

It is like Sunday school.

The young people also have their own meetings.

I most enjoy the singing.

Last term when schools closed we went to visit
our *gogo*, Grandmother Dawu, in the village.
We set out from the city very early in the morning.
We travelled in Father's car.
Mother said it was going to
be a very long journey to Matopo.
We had packed lots of food,
drinks and fruits to eat along the way.
It was fun to be on holiday.
We were looking forward to a
 good visit with Gogo Dawu.

We left the city behind.
There were fewer cars and people
along the road now.
The sky seemed clearer and the air fresher.

Finally, we came to Gogo's village.
It was nestling in a clearing, right off the main road.
There were five round mud huts with grass thatch.
Behind the homestead were big boulders
and rocks where Grandmother had dried
some of her grains from the fields.

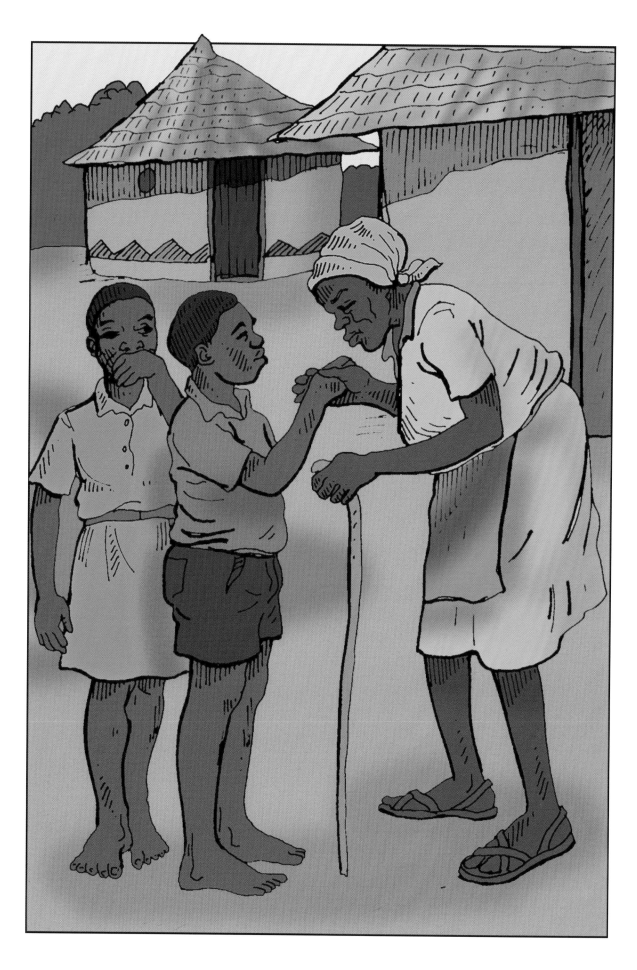

As soon as she heard the car,

Gogo came rushing out of one of the huts.

She ran out to meet our car.

She waved her arms and danced about.

She must have scared the cat and chickens.

They scattered and hid.

"O my, o my. Look who is here!"

She pulled me out of the car

and lifted me sky high.

When she planted me on my feet,

she smacked the back of my hand with a big kiss.

She did the same to Zenzo.

"O how lovely to have you!

And you have grown bigger.

Come, turn around. Let's see you some more!

O this is a happy day for me indeed!"

Great-grandmother came out more slowly.

She leaned on her stick and held out her hand.

We ran to her and got kissed again.

It was a good welcome for everyone.
Mother and Father got big handshakes.
The rest of the people in the village came out and
there was handshaking all round.

That evening we sat around the fire.
Grandmother served us *isitshwala* and *amasi*.
I had not wanted to sit around the fire.
I hated smoke in my eyes.
But Grandmother's fire was smoke free.
She used wood from iphane tree.

Many people were in the village.
Our cousins Ndaba and Sane
had also come to visit Grandmother.

Soon Sane and I became very good friends.
She took me rock sliding in the afternoons.
"This is how we do it. We take these branches
from *isikhukhukhu* tree. We lay them flat on this
rock with a slope. Take a ride on the branches and
Zoo—oo—oom! until you get to the bottom."
"Let me try it again. Zoooom–oom!
Goodie—it's fun."
"Zoo-oom. Here I come."

"Zoo . . . . .oo. . . . . .oom.
Here I come."

15

Life in the village is exciting.
My cousin and I work and
play together.

In the afternoons,
when it is too hot to work,
we do as we please.
We collect and
enjoy wild fruit.

The evenings are warm and cosy.

We sit around the fire.

We share stories or riddles.

Question:

"When I went to Jo'burg I was alone.

I was wearing a red shirt.

When I came back I had a khakhi suit.

There were many of us.

Who am I?"

Answer: "You are a groundnut."

Sometimes our *khokho* (great-grandmother)
tells a story. "A long time ago … when men and
animals spoke the same language … and the
rocks were soft enough to pinch … there lived…."

Or she starts, "A long time ago, before even your grandfather was born, strange people came to our land. They were white. They wore strange clothes.

They spoke a queer language and had strange habits. They told us about a carpenter called Jesus."

Sometimes it is a night for games
We play our favorite one
Bantwana, bantwana wozan'ekhaya
  (Children, children, come home)

Siyesaba
  (We are afraid)

Lesabani?
  (What are you afraid of?)

Izilwane
  (Lions)

Izilwane kudala zaphela du.
  (All the lions have been completely killed.)

Most interesting of all are the moonlit evenings.

There is no one by the fireside.

Everyone is out in the compound.

The children have all sorts of things lined up.

They sing, dance and act.

The adults laugh and clap.

"Haa haa haa. Hee hee hee! O yeah!"

Sometimes we count the stars.

We laugh at the moon.

"Gogola, tell us the story of the woman

who gathered firewood on Sunday.

Who punished her?

How was her picture put on the moon?"

We went to the Mission Church for Sunday
worship. One day there was news at church.
It made all the people very sad. Old Mfundisi
Khumalo had died. He was to be buried at
Matopo Mission.

Many people were at the funeral. They came from
all over Zimbabwe. They travelled in buses, lorries
and cars. Some came on bicycles. The rest walked.
Everyone said Khumalo was a good man. He told
many people about God.

One day as we were climbing the rocks we saw
Father's car coming along the winding road.
It was back to town for us.

Later in the day we had to run around.
"Catch it, catch it," mother cried as we
chased the rooster. It made a lovely last meal.

The next day we packed our bags.
We shook hands as we got into the car.
"Good-bye. Good-bye."
"Good-bye. See you next holiday."
"Bye! Bye!"
We waved until we could no longer
see the village.
We felt rather sad but we knew
we would come back.

The End